1

Iron is shiny too, not just silver.
Bronze is shiny too, not just gold.
But do they endure?

~

2

The firefly does not give light.
He just shows light.
Should he be paid for it?

~

3
I like my fingers.
They are all useful.
No matter how many fingers I have they all work together.

~

4
I am what you are.
And you are what I am.
And we are both what he is.
But he is not what we are.

~

5
Pots and cans want what's right.
But sticks and shields makes it straight.

6
Left and Right don't go together.
Right is right but Left is right too.

~

7
Pets like humans too much.
Wild animals know better.

~

8
Green is a good color.
Blue is better.
But Red is what it is desired.

~

9
Short or long?
Seen or unseen?
Clothes are all about the message.

~

10
The truth is naked.
Painting the truth with clothes.
Do you want to learn how to paint?

PATHWAY THROUGH THOUGHTS

A Travel Companion

CATALIN DAMIR

2018 First Edition

Author Preface

Traveling is never easy even when it is for pleasure. Time is lost on numerous tedious steps in airports or hotels and most of these steps include waiting time that is just wasted, usually in boring places.

Our random thoughts can be as rich as philosophy books but as a general rule we do not have the time to investigate them since life is quite busy. Sometimes we feel the burning desire to discover ourselves but we do not know where to start and we give up due to the lack of time and focus.

This book proposes to give the readers a chance to jump right into a peaceful meditation state and investigate these thoughts using the hidden tools of their experiences, culture, inner thoughts and religious or moral compass, so that at the end of the trip they can feel more enriched and satisfied than they were at the beginning of it.

Some thoughts can be looked at as guessing games and others are just crazy, mildly offensive or beautiful. Some thoughts have wisdom to share. Other thoughts might have the kind of wisdom that is harder to accept without an intellectual fight.

One advantage of sharing thoughts is that each assertion from these pages can be a great discussion starter with a friend or two or even with a stranger.

Please enjoy this literary travel companion and thoughts enhancer and dive into the wonderful world of random thoughts.

Catalin Damir

11
Art makes life better.
But life was already better.
We didn't know that before art.

~

12
Pens and sticks are not the same.
One has thought the other has wisdom.

~

13
Fancy is a mirror that smiles back at you.
Behind the mirror it's you.

~

14
Memories and drawers don't mix well, unless they are touched by shame.

~

15
Three lines and a dot.
Beauty is how you put them together.
Art.

16
"Be good!"
"Good Bye!"

~

17
Interesting is interesting.
You cannot make it dull.

~

18
I like. I like to like.
It feels good.

~

19
Harbors and ships stay on the sea.
But the sea moves.
Only the wind is faster.
Marry the wind.

~

20
Stars look like eyes piercing the night.
Love looks the same.

21
A kiss is something you desperately want even if the act itself doesn't make any sense whatsoever.

~

22
Flowers are the thoughts of plants.
They just leave them out in the open.

~

23
Fight and you will receive… lonely glory.

~

24
What you share is yourself.
What you ask is your greed.

~

25
You don't look through your eyes.
You look through your mind.
Change your mind.

26
Don't argue. All that energy can be used to build
pyramids and spaceships instead.

~

27
Secret energy comes from a secret place.
Make yourself a secret place and store energy.

~

28
Women and men are beautiful, alone or together.
Of course, together they make more beauty.
Beauty makes them laugh.

~

29
Aren't you happy already?
It is noon on the first day of your life.
How long do you need?

~

30
Run like you never ran before. Then stop.
What was that running about?

31
"You look good. You look in shape. You look amazing."
Wow, that is depressing. Let's all get an ice cream.
Life is too short for building looks.

~

32
Competition is good when you don't think about winning. But don't think about losing either.

~

33
Answering is not hard. Being right is hard.
What was first, the chicken or the egg? The chicken!
See?

~

34
Rationality and hard-work don't build dreams.
Irrationality and hard working might do the trick.

~

35
Cast the net into the water.
Then leave and let the fish decide.

36
Obvious is so obvious that it is boring.
Put a little mystery into it. Wow!

~

37
Some flowers are crushed.
Some make it to the vase.
Some are still free for all to look at.
Colors are better in the sun and the gentle wind moves them too.

~

38
You need to be happy?
Just smell the clean air. Find it first.

~

39
Bees are good.
Wasps are good too but they are less pleasant.
What if they marry?

~

40
Go find yourself.
But before that, learn about others.

41

The lake knows all about the stones in it. Stones don't know too much about the lake. But ducks do.

~

42

Thought travels faster than light.
Action travels faster than thought.
Remorse travels faster than action,
but not fast enough to stop the action.

~

43

Leaves are growing and you are looking at them wanting to be them.

~

44

Nature is cheerful, happy and beautiful.
In contrast, we are civilized.

~

45

Office work is exactly like open air work: one can space out indefinitely and not have a clue why he is there.

46
Time can go by without us noticing.
That's how we like it.

~

47
Animals listen carefully to what Man has to say to them. They're just not sure if they should believe him.

~

48
Careful, careful, you don't want that ego of yours to get hurt and become swollen.

~

49
Some like to share their thoughts with others. Some like to hide them. And some do both at the same time. The problem is that we are all on the same team.

~

50
No matter how much you want to stop the clock it is not going to work. Better put your energy into making it go faster. You will have that good feeling of accomplishment.

51
Being happy does not imply being humorous.
But it does make it easier for others when you joke.

~

52
Carpets are a thing of the past like innocence or childhood friendship.

~

53
Roads are always going to bring hope.
That is why they were built in the first place.

~

54
Civilization is desired by all until they figure out where it leads them.

~

55
Why do we work and stress?
It is because we are stuck with a body which is very demanding.

56
Without work there is no civilization.
Without civilization there is no work.
The effort however will always be around.

~

57
The World is an illusion. Is it really?
Then why can I not think of anything else?

~

58
Clouds are wonderful to look at. Sometimes they do tricks. I wonder if they do them willingly.

~

59
Before, the World was without end. Now it is not.
Instead the Universe is now without an end.
But for how long?

~

60
"Live and let live."
"Yeah right.
With this attitude how am I to conquer the world?"
Maybe it is better not to conquer it...

61
Listening and seeing gives you empathy.
But you need power to change the world.
Once you have power you don't listen and see anymore.

~

62
When I was a child I was really happy and sometimes really unhappy. Now that I am old enough I don't feel much anymore.

~

63
Skyscrapers are the new pyramids.
You can see that by the slaves going in and out of them.

~

64
Poverty is never deserved.
Neither is wealth.

~

65
Look at the natural grass.
Green, tall, smooth and beautiful.
Now cut it! Isn't that better?
Let's do the same with all the animals.

66
Food tastes good as long as you think on it. Once your mind goes away it tastes like nothing.

~

67
Spoons and forks shine on a table.
In the street they are dirty and broken.

~

68
I see a horse, I dream of adventure.
I see a cow, I dream of food.
I see a bird, I dream of freedom.
I see a human and I wake up from my dream state as fast as I can.

~

69
"Rapid company assessment...
Benefits of proposed program...
Policy and regulatory initiative..."
"No more techno babble. Just steal the company already!"

~

70
Daycare memories feel like they are from another life.

71

Animal rights are something the insects can only dream of. But they don't have cute eyes to get it.

~

72
What are colors?
They exist only because of our eyes.

~

73
"Beauty is in the eye of the beholder."
"You mean in the heart or soul… of the beholder."
"There is no such thing as soul!"
"Then there is no such thing as beauty!"

~

74
Sadducees do not believe in an immortal soul.
Pharisees do not believe in the Son of God.
Poor people just hope both exist:
One for justice, One for mercy.

~

75
The lesson of life is that there is no lesson.
There is just a test at the end.

76
School is good until you remember that you were once free.

~

77
Wealth is something that does not really exist for someone that has only one body for about 80-90 years. Don't lose your life for it.

~

78
Mathematically speaking Life is an impossible equation. We hope that everything will make sense after Life.

~

79
Being rational does not imply being wise.

~

80
Try not to impose your truth on people.
Let the Truth do that.

81
Happiness is something you can achieve in this life only by renouncing the pursuit of it.

~

82
The engine was not made for the road.
We made the road for it.
Horses are happy that they are not abused anymore.

~

83
Even the thought of work requires rest.

~

84
Sleep is not rest. It is fuel.
To rest you need to be awake.

~

85
The stars still look mysterious even if we already know what they are.

86
Enigma and Mystery are not the same thing.
One can be solved and disappear, the other one will stay around and enchant us.

~

87
The spider web is just a tool for gathering food.
Other than that it is pure art.

~

88
Work. Play. Rest.
If you remove Work then Rest becomes an annoyance.

~

89
The reward of work is dignity, not money.
If you just want money then you better forget about work as it is slowing you down in getting it.

~

90
Go and find your happiness in this world, but don't forget to stop when you find it.

91
Wars are an opportunity for our leaders to show us that we were always leaderless.

~

92
The hero will fight for the others because he thinks that they are worth saving. The others don't join the hero in the fight because they do not share the same opinion about themselves.

~

93
Being rude is a virtue only in an upside down Universe.
I must be in the wrong Universe.
Does anybody know where the Exit?

~

94
The real secret for successful chocolate is sugar not cocoa and milk. Of course without cocoa and milk, plain sugar is boring.

~

95
If you want to succeed in business don't listen to anybody's good or bad opinion.
If you want to succeed in spiritual endeavors listen to everybody and draw your conclusions.

96
Before asking for inspiration first answer the question: what do you want to do with it?

~

97
Prayers are words from a language that it is not spoken on Earth.

~

98
The Sun is a beautiful star. It is also the most useful star around. Without usefulness, beauty cannot be admired. Without beauty, usefulness loses its meaning.

~

99
Without this planet, humanity would be reduced to nothingness.

~

100
Astronauts proved that we cannot survive long enough anywhere else than Earth. Of course, dreamers will have different opinions about this.

101

The pocket calculator is the most useful invention in history. Unfortunately it got completely overshadowed by the game console.

~

102

If you want to be useful do not ask what people need. Instead ask what people are dreaming about.

~

103

Oranges and bananas can't be counted the same as apples and pears. They are from different latitudes.

~

104

Stupid thoughts can be as valuable as genius thoughts. Certainly they feel like that at certain times.

~

105

Love is a matter of taste.
It does not need to be explained.

106
When you are young, you desire.
When you are old, you desire to desire.

~

107
If you want to be young at heart let yourself be as ridiculous as possible.

~

108
The fight is not against food.
The fight is against us.
Who can defeat himself and win?

~

109
Our stomach is not at fault. It is our hands and mouth that are the conspirators.

~

110
If you have twenty fingers, one nose, two eyes, one mouth, and two ears it is indecent to complain about life. If you have less, don't get bothered by numbers.

111
Long life, many opportunities.
Short life, fewer opportunities.
You need only one to make your life count.

~

112
Boringness cannot be conquered while we are still in this Universe.

~

113
The happiness of a child in his first days alive is due to his belief that he is in Heaven. The moment he finds out that he is on Earth he smiles with half of his mouth and starts to build up patience until this is over.

~

114
If we could be immortal and could experience all that we want in this material life will that be satisfying enough? And if it is not, then why even bother to experience all that is here.

~

115
Duck, Duck, Goose! I don't even know if I want to be the duck or the goose.

116
Worrying is the daily routine of regular people. Not worrying at all can be achieved only by the worst criminals or holiest saints.

~

117
Trying to escape justice is like trying to get away in school by cheating the whole year. However, the year-end exam cannot be cheated.

~

118
All opportunities in life are dependent on luck. However afterlife opportunities are always a matter of choice. There are no opportunists in Heaven… unless they repent.

~

119
If you seek glory and recognition, then Earth is the wrong place to look for it. Here even the most successful of us is envied and unappreciated. The same thing happens to the least successful of us too.

~

120
Try not to think how about large the Universe is. You might get claustrophobic.

121
Religion will never disappear as long as there is a God to worship. And there is always one in us.

~

122
If you want to have your mind amazed then ask God why He created the fly, the rat and the virus.
The answers must be shocking in the least.

~

123
History is full of inspired people. But it avoids saying who inspired them.

~

124
Drugs are one of Gods way of telling us that behind matter there is an idea.

~

125
What we call Nature is just a bunch of objects put together in an organized way. Occasionally we see the way some of them work together, but most of the time we are blind to their interactions.

126
Philosophical ideas are a way of expressing our sheer panic of where, who and what are we.

~

127
Wealth is desired by many but once we have it nobody knows exactly what we are supposed to do with it. So we just get silly with it.

~

1*28*
The poor do not need wealth.
Nor do they need sympathy.
All they need is some time to get on their feet.
But time is money. Give them some.

~

129
Helping somebody is as hard as helping yourself.

~

130
Dreams are not here to entertain us.
They are trying to tell us something.
Whoever is sending them should be aware of our analytical prowess and just speak to us plainly.

131
Patience is only virtue if it is not mixed with laziness.

~

132
The entire fabric of humanity is filled with laziness. This is actually good since the lazy are interested in the highest efficiency.

~

133
Creativity is the only good pastime in this corner of the Universe.

~

134
Creativity and impatience go hand in hand. Even if it takes 50 years to finish your creation you will be impatient every hour of every day of every year of it.

~

135
Express yourself but only the good parts. We already know all the bad parts.

136
Don't brag too often about your weaknesses.
But don't forget about them either.

~

137
Don't give advice like the one I am giving just now.
Subtlety is a sign of refinement.

~

138
The Archvillain is not at the same spiritual level as
the Hero. But he secretly desires to be.

~

139
The weakness of a Hero is that deep inside he knows
he is just a normal human being and he is afraid that
he might revert at any moment to that level.
Or maybe this is his only strength.

~

140
Being unafraid is as easy as being afraid, but much
more dangerous.

141
Pushing yourself to the limits might be the last thing you do. So do it right.

~

142
Bad times can teach you many good things. But somehow we don't come out wiser from them.

~

143
Awareness is paying enough attention to something that did not happened yet. More than that is called paranoia.

~

144
Politics is the art of lying continuously to yourself that you are remotely useful to society.

~

145
The only useful politician is the one that in a moment of conscience publishes all the dirt he knows about himself and all the other politicians.

146
Power is not the most desired dream of a politician. Respect is. But he cannot get any respect until he uses power on his subjects.

~

147
Most people seem to confuse respect with fame or inspiring fear in others, two of the worst weaknesses of humanity.

~

148
If you want respect first you have to understand who you are. Once you do that you will be the first to renounce it.

~

149
Introspection is the only weapon we have against losing our humanity.

~

150
Leaves look with interest to the sun every day and talk about it. The sun is alone and does not know them.

151
Flying and swimming help us forget that we are just humans. Walking in space does the opposite.

~

152
We know that all computers are broken.
We just don't know what is broken in them and how to fix it completely.

~

153
We should be afraid of robots.
Just look at who created them.

~

154
Technology is our attempt to prove ourselves to the Creator. Unfortunately this is not the challenge He has given us.

~

155
The most depressive prison is a city.
In there, the prisoners build their own walls and then look over them crying.

156
There are two perfect shapes: the Cube and the Sphere. But only one shape is visible everywhere in our Universe. The other shape must be from another Universe.

~

157
We are not used to living in a three dimensional world. That is why we are always looking for the lost dimension.

~

158
We are all failures.
Some of us don't like to say it loudly.
Some of us don't even know the meaning of the word.

~

159
War is like hunting except that you're lying that you have to do it.

~

160
The hunter can be a villain or a saviour.
It depends on whose side he is on.

161
The army will always be the second most respected institution on this planet. What else can you do when dealing with armed men? Lucky for us, even they are afraid of something or Someone.

~

162
Try to educate yourself while you can. The way things are, this planet wants as much muscle and as little brain as possible.

~

163
Work should be split into two categories: Pleasure and Survival. Both are reasons to be called lucky when you get a job.

~

164
The hungrier you are the clearer you see your priorities.

~

165
Renunciation is a sign of advanced spirituality. Evil people are every bit as spiritual as the saints.

166
Spirituality is a misunderstood term.
It never implied good intentions.

~

167
Being *good* is a choice distinguished entirely from *not being bad*. There is an element of passivity in not being something.

~

168
We know what is Bad.
But, what is Good?

~

169
Making good food brings back good memories.

~

170
The bears, the wolves and the sharks play the villains in many movies. I hope they get paid damages. The bunnies and the field mice are laughing all the way to the bank.

171
Movies are a simulation of the Roman Colosseum.
That is why whatever they show is still socially acceptable.

~

172
It's easy to be sarcastic or ironic.
It does not involve any new ideas.

~

173
Having an idea is exhilarating.
That is why it is not permitted in an office.

~

174
Laughing has nothing to do with enjoying.

~

175
Most of lies cannot be preemptively identified simply because they started out as truths.

176
Bugs are insects that we want to crush.

~

177
Poets don't like to talk right.
Luckily for them we like the way they talk.

~

178
Worms dream of flying.
Once they fly they dream of eating poop.

~

179
Flying is not about destinations.
It is about freedom.

~

180
You fish from a boat while looking at stars.
The fish in the water are looking at you and wonder what you are thinking about. Some of them will look at you from the plate later.

181
Extreme old age is the most indecent experiment.
We are lucky it is temporary.

~

182
Punishment should be followed by Forgiveness, or else it should be renamed Destruction.

~

183
White moon. Yellow moon. Red moon.
Same basic colors as street lights.
Do they have the same meaning?

~

184
"Relax now. The worst has passed."
What a lie! It can always become worse than what it was before.

~

185
Get your priorities right.
Breathing comes first.

186
Seasons are here to show a different perspective of the same place. Sometimes a place cannot be improved no matter the perspective.

~

187
Dogs are defending us just because they got used to being fed by us.

~

188
Culture is not required when building a career. Not even for a career in culture.

~

189
Intellectuals are useless until you run out of ideas.

~

190
Culture is not achieved through learning art, music, history and literature. You just need to be interested in truth.

191
If you want to know things, you need a book.
If you want to do things right, you need a master.
If you want to succeed where others have failed, you need yourself.

~

192
Silence can be as sweet as music and as annoying as noise.

~

193
Balancing is our constant concern.

~

194
Peace of mind is a step behind peace of heart.

~

195
Creating something good and beautiful is nothing less than bliss for everyone.

196
To create you need only will, not gifts.

~

197
Destruction cannot be called creative.
One is too absorbed by himself when doing it.

~

198
When travelling you might be tempted by loneliness and when not travelling you might be tempted by despair. Both these feelings reflect a false reality.

~

199
Looking at a fire you can observe the flames dancing before your eyes. Look but don't touch.

~

200
Meditation comes as a glove when travelling.
Don't waste it.

201
True value is measured in time spent meditating.

~

202
Fire and wood have a great relationship.
Unfortunately it is consumed too quickly.
Getting the right mix can take a lifetime.

~

203
Civilized people live in houses.
Uncivilized people live everywhere.

~

204
There is a large variety of colors in light. Together they form white, which is not a color.

~

205
Contrary to what is believed by some, good and evil are not sides of the same coin. Rather they are two different coins from divergent banks. One bank is already bankrupt. The other bank is poor in coins.

206
Physical work is good for you.
What is good for you might not be good for others.

~

207
Comedy should not be confused with sarcasm and irony. These two are belligerent in scope while comedy is peaceful.

~

208
Children's games are idiotic and that is why they are fun.

~

209
Adults pretend to understand children but the matter of fact is that they do not come even close to that level of intellectual freedom.

~

210
Trains, cars, boats and planes are not just travelling vehicles. They are peaceful homes, public places, busy offices and tombs, all in one package at the same time. What a marvel of modern sociology.

211
Going uphill or downhill wear out shoes in equal measure.

~

212
A blank page for an author can be as inspiring as a full page for a reader.

~

213
When you are begging on your knees your height no longer matters.

~

214
Ideas are not worth fighting for.
However, some ideas are worth fighting against.

~

215
Beauty is in the eye of the beholder.
Property is much more stable than that.

216
Money does not bring happiness.
That is because whoever has it looks for superficial satisfaction instead of what will really make them happy.

~

217
The crayon is more interesting than the pen. When not writing, it can create art. However, you need a pen to sign documents. What a bore!

~

218
Adventurers are people that did not believe that the world is boring.

~

219
Being an explorer was one of the bloodiest enterprises of the 16th century. It took some times to make it as respectable as it is today.

~

220
Poor people don't discover new lands.
As always you need to be already filthy rich for that to happen.

221
Fame and Art are as close as War and Peace.

~

222
To be able to call yourself a great artist you first need to be a true human being. There are no true human beings alive. However, there are many that are dead.

~

223
True Artists are the ones that give something to others that they never knew existed.

~

224
Being an artist involves working with beauty. But beauty is false if it is not truthful. And there is no truth to be found on Earth.

~

225
Artists are just cracked doors to another world that doesn't belong to them.

226
Working with music and colors makes you nothing more than a worker. Artists do not work.

~

227
If you want to become an artist then you need to forget about all the art done before you.
But it is advisable to learn all you can before you forget about it.

~

228
Art is always beautiful. If it is not beautiful, then it is just a political statement.

~

229
A good painter has the same sense of volume as a sculptor. A good sculptor has the same sense of light and shadows as a painter.

~

230
Paintings and sculptures send all the message to our eyes. Music always keeps some of its mysteries.

231
We do not treat nature the way it treats us.

~

232
The pollution of nature is our inability to deal with what we want versus what we need.

~

233
The way we already are is reflected in the way we want to be.

~

234
People of all ages should be treated with respect since age will change for all of them at some point.

~

235
There are no arguments left in front of a gun.
The gun already lost the dialog.

236
Winning no matter the consequences can be accepted only if the cause is good. The cause can be good only if all mankind benefits from it. You must be from Heaven to know what is good for all mankind.

~

237
Organized religion can be improved by science. But science should not become organized religion.

~

238
Religion versus Science is like knowledge versus materials. You need both knowledge and materials to build something.

~

239
Freedom is such a mysterious concept that even angels did not get it right.

~

240
Children are the wisest on this planet. They still see the world for what it is.

241

Childhood can be heaven on Earth if the children are just left alone to play.

~

242

School is a place where you learn to obey. Learning is treated as a secondary goal there.

~

243

If teachers seem to like power more than teaching, then they should be called by a different name.

~

244

Learning is about Freedom and Power. Power and Freedom are enemies that one must choose from.

~

245

Intuition and rationality can be best of friends or the worst of enemies.

246
Understanding new things does not lead automatically to accepting them.

~

247
Politics are not about what party is more acceptable or what kind of government we can have. It is about people that don't want to work and that ask for our money.

~

248
The difference between homeless people and politicians is that the homeless cannot find proper work while politicians don't want to find proper work.

~

49
Rich people are not happier than poor people. They just pretend they are.

~

250
Whoever thinks fame implies true respect lives a lie.

251
Vacation is the time we spend dreaming of freedom in the prison courtyard. The fence is still there at the end of it.

~

252
The future of our civilization is more complex morally and technologically than we now hope to be.

~

253
Civilization is a crust on top of this planet. And it gets thinner by the minute.

~

254
After all will be said and done the matter of fact is that this Universe is a *finite* object. We need *infinite* resources.

~

255
The divide between rich and poor is actually a divide between those who still experience the luxury of civilization and those who don't anymore.

256
There is this lie that is said over and over: "The spirit is willing but the body is not". The truth is the spirit is not willing as well.

~

257
The forest does not need saving. It just needs be left alone.

~

258
The biggest divide in human history was the birth of "us" and "them".

~

259
This planet was always up for grabs. But now our fingers are starting to feel the end of the cookie bag.

~

260
Being cheerful in times of need is not madness. It is just a sign of knowing something the others don't.

261
If you want all people to get along then they should all acknowledge that they are equal in desires and needs.

~

262
Equality is not something you can negotiate. Either you are or you are not equal.

~

263
The concept of equality is not new. It is actually the oldest around. But as in the first days of man, this issue is still not solved today due to selfishness.

~

264
We can save this world as easy as saying what is mine is yours.

~

265
Motivational speeches do not work unless you are already motivated.

266
Be careful not to become tyrannical when you are enforcing good.

~

267
Good requires a higher effort from us than evil. That is why we invented half-good.

~

268
Our life can be spent on living or on preparation for living.

~

269
The economic truth of all time is that more is not better.

~

270
The scientific truth of all time is that a lot of what we know today is the laughing stock of what we will know tomorrow.

271
The technological truth of all time is that without it people will still live in the woods but with it soon there will be no more woods.

~

272
The politic truth of all time is that the moment we elect somebody to talk for us we lose our voice.

~

273
The military truth of all time is that for most men dialog is less interesting than fighting.

~

274
Nature is all about details.
We are about half-thought broad concepts.

~

275
It is an unlucky thing that animals don't have the ability to speak up. It would save us a lot of hypocrisy.

276
No matter how smart we will become we will never be able to create something completely new.

~

277
Everything in the Universe is of no real value since it is limited by time.

~

278

The Universe will die due to entropy. What can mankind do to survive it?

~

279
True value has to be immortal value or else there is no point in acquiring it since temporary value will lose all value at some point in time.

~

280
The proof that immortality exist is the fact that we can dream about it.

281
We are all immortals living in a mortal Universe.

~

282
Trying to find meaning in life can take more than your lifespan.

~

283
The stomach is one of those parts of our body that has a mind of its own. Lucky for us it accepts bribes.

~

284
Our need to replicate in art everything from the known Universe is curious indeed.
We should want to see the unknown.

~

285
If you count the years or months of your life you will find them to be many. If you count the seconds you will find them to be just a few.

286
Some build pyramids, some look at them.
Most don't care about them at all.

~

287
Making money feels good. Spending it feels better.
Giving it feels the best.

~

288
"Beauty is in the eye of the beholder."
Of course, it is actually the mind that is the judge of beauty and it can be taught to see it.

~

289
If you are color blind you did are not missing anything. There are a lot of good black & white movies.

~

290
If an image is worth a thousand words and a movie is worth a thousand images, then a good book is worth a thousand movies since nothing can beat imagination.

291
Actors are not afraid to show you who you really are.

~

292
From all the arts, movies are the most appreciated by the general public since we lost the Colosseum rights.

~

293
If you can choose between art and life then go with art. It will be less of a disappointment.

~

294
You cannot choose art before life.
Art is about life.

~

295
Exploring oneself can be as close to auto destruction as ever.

296
For most of us "Improve yourself" is better advice than "Be yourself".

~

297
Writing can be either a repository of eternal wisdom or a storage of temporary data.

~

298
When reading a book your imagination is intertwined with that of the writer.
What if the writer is God?

~

299
Childhood play is the closest we got to pure entertainment.

~

300
If you want to be entertained first you need to laugh at yourself.

301
Kings could not laugh at themselves without danger. So they hired a court jester for that purpose.

~

302
Guns are banned for children for safety reasons. Unfortunately the ban does not extend to immature people.

~

303
Peace cannot be achieved through arms. But it can be kept that way.

~

304
If you don't want war them make sure peace is enforced.

~

305
Peace can be used for war but war cannot be used for peace. However, defending yourself is not war.

306
World peace can be achieved only through world tyranny. The other way is divine intervention.

~

307
Tyranny is perpetual war disguised as peace.

~

308
World peace is as easy as asking all mankind to not desire anything.

~

309
As long as there are weapons in this world war is just a shot away.

~

310
Running along is not the same as running with.

311
Either you say something or you don't. Such is the nature of opinions.

~

312
The world has improved at the same time that it has regressed.

~

313
You don't know that you have really improved yourself until you find out where the direction of your improvement leads.

~

314
If you go to battle make sure you know all your enemies.

~

315
Once you are in battle gear make sure you know where your friends are.

316
A battle can be just a battle or the whole war.

~

317
Talking is more important than weapons until the war starts. Find out if the enemy wants war before negotiating.

~

318
Before you negotiate make sure war is not the only option.

~

319
Ultimate war is like ultimate peace: a dream for idealists.

~

320
When an idealist thinks that there is a chance to fulfill his ideal he becomes like a bomb looking for a match.

321
The world was more hurt by idealists than helped by them.

~

322
A good negotiator is better than your best fighter or weapon system.

~

323
Half of the negotiation is already achieved if you know exactly what you want.

~

324
Before you ask for help see if you need it.
This cannot be repeated too many times.

~

325
Giving help to others is honorable, unless the goal is negative.

326
Stars look smaller than planets to the naked eye. However, they are not.

~

327
If at some point in time man will walk on other planets, he should never forget how he treated his first planet.

~

328
If Earth is a ship then we are worse than rats. Rats do not cause the sinking of their own ship.

~

329
Planting a tree in front of your house does not solve the issue of clean air or habitats for animals, birds and insects. You need a forest for that.

~

330
Protecting forests should be more important than all other policies since without them we are all dead. Try to tell that to a business man.

331
The sound of a forest cannot be replicated by sound devices no more than the sound of your mother.

~

332
Unless we become vegetarians, the last animal we will eat is going to be biped and intelligent.

~

333
This planet is the ultimate death row cell and there is only one thing you can do in a cell: make friends with God.

~

334
It does not matter that the sky is blue if it is covered with clouds. Clear the clouds.

~

335
The most profitable industry to invest in these days is energy. However, we have abundant energy all around us that we do not use.

336
It is not an accident that the weapons industry is one of the largest in this scientific age. It is needed to prevent real progress.

~

337
Before rulers were fighting rulers for their people. Now rulers are just fighting the people.

~

338
Politics is a dirty game. We just think we can clean it a bit with our vote.

~

339
There is no real power on Earth. We are all slaves. Some slaves are mindless about their situation and think they are rulers.

~

340
Helping others is never out of fashion.
It is as cool as ever.

341
When you grow older, things start to make sense but by then you already lose interest.

~

342
Old is not the new young.
Young should be the new old.

~

343
The spirit can never be old because it cannot look into a mirror.

~

344
Travel and see the world.
But don't forget that the world can see you too.

~

345
Travelling is an opportunity for good behavior.

346
When travelling pay attention to small details.
It might be the only things that you will remember with pleasure.

~

347
Without historic knowledge of the places you visit, traveling is just an expensive getaway.

~

348
Travelling can be as boring as staying in your house.
It all depends on your attitude.

~

349
Landmarks are great photo opportunities. Don't travel only in photos.

~

350
With the proper book you can have meaningful experiences even in a line at the airport.

351
Religion is not about God,
God is about religion.

~

352
If man invented religion then civilization is not required to exist since only brute power is important in that equation.

~

353
Reneging on one religion is possible without shattering civilization, reneging on all religions is not.

~

354
Civilization is deeply linked to our moral code. If the moral code is getting weak then the bonds keeping civilization are getting weaker and even in danger of breaking.

~

355
What a religious man can do to another man is bound to the moral code he receives through his religion. An atheist's moral code is either a surprise or an unknown.

356
Good and Evil are the only true religious words since they speak of absolute authority. If you drop religion then you better drop these words altogether.

~

357
Both the religious man and the atheist are afraid of God.

~

358
The woman equation is as unknown as the man equation. But we are supposed to get along just fine.

~

359
Men will always be impressed by women.
This is not negotiable.

~

360
Marriage was never only about two people.
Society is involved too.

361
A tough marriage is something hard to bear.
However, that is where your character gets tested.

~

362
In ideal conditions any man can have a successful marriage with any woman. I love the word "ideal". It is so out of this world.

~

363
Liberal marriages are pushing the institution to its limits. This is where we see that a word loses its meaning if you change its primary goal.

~

364
Marriage is a union with the goal of making and educating children in a safe environment. Everything else is economic unions or pleasure partnerships.

~

365
Couples can hate each other.
It is allowed as long as they are in love.

366
If marriage is just a social contract then by all means, who needs more contracts in their life?

~

367
I can never imagine a world where there are no married people. However, such a world already exists.

~

368
The most prominent feminist activist is Jesus Christ. He promised that in Heaven women will be no different than men.

~

369
Men fight women out of fear that women have everything they need to win without a fight.

~

370
Women desire to be equal with men, and men desire to be equal with God. One of them has a chance.

371
Man and women are what makes this planet
interesting to women and men.

~

372
Between man and women should be always a place
for a child (or more).

~

373
Men have a duty to protect women.
It is only fair since they were already protected by
them for a critical nine months.

~

374
If God created different kinds of human beings He
must've done it to teach us respect for differences.

~

375
If somebody thinks of themselves as different from
others it does not make it so. If someone is indeed
different it does not matter what the others think.

376
Having a different personality than mainstream society will always be seen as special.
It is the nature of herds.

~

377
Society is a herd that may or may not listen to the shepherd.

~

378
For a true religious person freedom of thought is catalyzed by his religious choice. But many of the theists are not true religious men.

~

379
Theists and atheists are all flawed human beings.

~

380
If somebody tells you that you are different, they are probably right.

381
Being different is like being chosen.
It is an opportunity for greatness in the right hands.

~

382
Being the same is as safe as being in the train with others. Sometimes trains derail.

~

383
Rationality is not our strongest cognitive skill.
However, we rely on it more than the other skills.
Memory should be used more often.

~

384
Learning can be difficult if you don't see what you need it for.

~

385
If you need to learn something then first learn how to learn.

386
Waiting for an airplane is as exciting as waiting for a spaceship. That is how people thought about waiting for trains only two centuries ago. Before that there were horses and boats for as long as we remember.

~

387
All transport technology is fairly new and exciting and it is a proof to how fast people get bored by new things.

~

388
The digital era is just starting.
Some are already fed up with it.

~

389
Time cannot be turned back.
This applies to technology as well.

~

390
Adapting to technology is not just a requirement.
It is also fun.

391
Technology does not have to be useful to be accepted, just trendy.

~

392
For every app there is a market, mostly tiny ones.

~

393
In digital era ideas fly easier than before. So easy in fact that some ideas fly directly out of the window.

~

394
The digital market moves faster than product ability to get a fair trial.

~

395
Our brains are already full with information. What we need is to let go of this information in a safe spot.

396
First there was the letter, then it was the telegraph, then it was the phone. After that it was the email and now it is the instant message. What is the use if you don't have anything interesting to say?

~

397
Privacy these days is quite suspicious.
There was a time when it was revered.

~

398
All digital communication is already obsolete.
We are trembling with excitement for the next level.

~

399
Silence allows us to hear our thoughts.
That is why we should all look for it.

~

400
Our mind has so much to tell us.
But it is interrupted many times.
We need to schedule time aside for it.

401
Give us time and we will give you value.

~

402
There are so many things to do.
Don't choose only one.
You might get good at it and lose yourself.

~

403
Robots are things that we invent to occupy our nightmares.

~

404
Drones are as much robots as a fork is.

~

405
The first real robots will have the ability to make us take pity on them.

406
It is impossible to achieve Artificial Intelligence while we don't know first what Intelligence is.

~

407
If we think our brain is just a network of neurons then the most we can obtain is digital networks. Networks don't have new thoughts.

~

408
Our dream to become a superhero is now achievable. You just need to choose the character.

~

409
Robots are another word for slaves.
It implies the same emotional disconnection.
This time around we are on the right track.

~

410
All movies about sentient robots forget the fact that this is not what we are trying to create. Movie makers should get with the program.

411
Robots are an endless discussion topic since they deal with our true meaning of life: to skip work.

~

412
The question if there is life on another planet is less interesting than what happens after death.

~

413
The Universe is limited. Our mind is not.
That is because it is prepared for something else.

~

414
We should not achieve positive thinking through ignorance.

~

415
Negative thinking will always lead to depression.
Positive thinking takes longer to get there.

416
Hope is a concept that was dropped on Earth from Heaven.

~

417
Our mind is not built to think small thoughts. That is why we are including small thoughts in a larger matrix.

~

418
When working with others remember that they are only human. And so are you.

~

419
If you want to solve issues you must understand them first. When you truly understand an issue the solution appears by default.

~

420
If you want to have an extremely good evolution in a company prepare yourself for devolution in humanity.

421
It seems rulers don't know other recipes than an omelet. And they often use too many eggs.

~

422
Being rude will never gain you respect. In fact you lose whatever respect you possessed. But then again, maybe respect is not something you are interested in to begin with.

~

423
Politeness without empathy is another form of rudeness.

~

424
Empathy is the highest form of a relationship. Even lovers do not get to it often.

~

425
The only issue on this planet is the lack of empathy. All goes downhill from there.

426
The mathematical concept hardest to enforce is "one plus one equals two".

~

427
Another concept is "lion's share". Although it deals with numbers it has nothing to do with mathematics.

~

428
In a perfect world one plus one always equals two. In our world we want that all absolute truth to become relative truth.

~

429
Death is not a relative truth. It cannot be interpreted from a subjective point of view.

~

430
Life is not a relative truth.
Only the various use of life falls in that category.

431
Charity is the economic activity with the highest return of profit. However this return might not be in the form of money.

~

432
When dealing with corporate profit, if the highest economic thought is that of cutting your fellow man from getting his bread, then what is the lowest economic thought: Empathy?

~

433
Once Justice is defeated in a state of law all economic systems can be abused by thieves.

~

434
The only way Justice can protect its territory is through absolute transparency.

~

435
Government should be as transparent as thin glass. Behind any shadow there is a thief.

436
Capitalist governments are controlled immediately after the election by thieves.
Communist governments are controlled by thieves way before the election begins.

~

437
Communists do not understand human corruption. That is why all their governments end up in feudal ruling.

~

438
Capitalists understand human corruption and act accordingly to it. That is why all their governments end up dirty.

~

439
Socialists understand human corruption and pretend to prevent it. That is why all their governments end up being a bad joke.

~

440
Theocrats understand human corruption and take measure only on lower levels leading to more abuse than ever. One of their achievements is killing God.

441
There is total failure in dealing with corruption from all political systems. However, Anarchy is not the answer.

~

442
Anarchy comes with only one promise: total Freedom. That is a promise Anarchy cannot keep for long.

~

443
Slavery is the lowest step towards emancipation with Anarchy being the last.

~

444
Anarchy is just one warlord away from Slavery.

~

445
Without justice on all levels, society will continue to fluctuate indefinitely between one social system to another.

446
The political vicious circle can be improved only through continuous education.

~

447
Love is the reward for reaching all virtues.

~

448
Virtues are all equal among each other.
Sins are not.

~

449
Many of us do not like the word "sin".
Apparently that is a sin in itself.

~

450
Sin exists only in relationship with Perfection.
But does Perfection exist? This is a question to which many do not like the answer.

451
The only thing easier than building a virtue is losing it. However we are allowed to re-start building it as many times as we want.

~

452
Leaving home can be exhilarating.
Returning to it is no less emotional.

~

453
You know you are ready for life when you are not afraid of the future, whatever it might be.

~

454
The young will dream of maturity.
Once there, they dream of childhood.

~

455
Optimism is ingrained in the young heart.
That is why the only advice you should accept is to keep your heart young.

456
Starting again cannot be harder than starting for the first time.

~

457
Optimism should not become merchandise.

~

458
The hope for a better life should not depart from you even at the end of it.

~

459
Happiness is fused with hope.

~

460
Optimism is the highest form of hope since it does not need proof of it.

461
The only thing you can lose from optimism is pessimism.

~

462
Pessimism should not be confused with wisdom.
It lacks the element of courage.

~

463
Wisdom can be brave even when not acting.

~

464
Bravery and Pride can look the same for a while.
But only Bravery goes on until the end.

~

465
If you are looking for your way in life then don't stop at your skills.

466
Improving yourself should not feel coerced. You just need to recognize early enough that it is the only thing you really care about.

~

467
Vegetables and fruits have all the nutrients we need. That is not why we eat them.

~

468
Meat is not required in our alimentation. Still, it is the most consumed aliment.

~

469
All recipes are creative ways of eating the same thing over and over.

~

470
Playing chess is like playing poker except that your pieces are visible all the time.

471
Algorithm is a complicated word for mathematical creativity. If you understand it you can paint with numbers.

~

472
Einstein had the idea but he needed
Planck to make it mathematically possible.

~

473
All you need to travel faster than light is to understand how the Universe works.
Easier said than done.

~

474
If we will ever travel from one star to another let's hope we will never forget where the Sun is.

~

475
Once we can travel within the Universe the next question to answer will be what is beyond it.

476
If there is a limit to this Universe then we will find it. If there is not, then we found God.

~

477
What God has in common with the Universe is that He is both harsh and merciful to the point of extreme contrast.

~

478
Science and Technology were born from our need for absolute answers. But once we receive some answers we decide that they are not absolute and we look for more.

~

479
If this Universe is not enough for us why do we think another one is going to be satisfying?

~

480
Sleeping is the ultimate form of trust. When we do it we lose all control for a critical part of time.

481
Sleep was invented so we can have a piece of heavenly rest available every day.

~

482
One day our next dream is going to be the beginning of another life.

~

483
Dreams are one way of trying to escape into a perfect reality.

~

484
Dreams are proofs that a better reality is possible.

~

485
Cover your mouth, your eyes and your ears.
Now listen to your soul.

486
Snails would like to be fast, birds would like to have a house.

~

487
Poor and rich are poor.

~

488
Wealth that you cannot use or keep forever is not yours.

~

489
Using wealth is like using a car.
That's why you should be very careful with it.

~

490
There are no rich people, we are all on death row.
Some get the last meal, some not.

491
If you think God exists, be a saint.
If you think He does not exist be a devil for there is nobody to make you accountable.

~

492
Don't lie to yourself that you are good. I can find a hundred reasons at any time why you are not good.

~

493
Doing good things is like doing bad things.
It requires passion and commitment.

~

494
If you want to fight evil don't be passive.
Passivity is the smallest step towards evil.

~

495
Unless you are a professional, don't be hyperactive when fighting evil. It makes you look sloppy.

496
Evil and Good are like two fighters that are circling each other and looking for weaknesses.
When they finally act it must be decisive.

~

497
Growing up you might have dreams and hopes.
Do not lose them for they keep you alive.

~

498
Melons are green on the outside and red on the inside. One might say they are not done yet judging by the outer color.

~

499
If you run from something be sure that it will wait for you at the end of your run.

~

500
Controversial subjects can change from one era to another, from one country to another, from one religion to another.

501
What one man considers good another considers bad. The question is how can you make them safe for each other.

~

502
Respect is the only medicine for all of society's wounds.

~

503
If you want to live together in an open society then you will need to iron out most of the issues.

~

504
The most dangerous members of society are the young ones. They are also our brightest hope.

~

505
Changing the world can be done more easily than thought. Changing it in the right direction is what is hard.

506
Communication between people can be improved.
Cooperation is another ball game.

~

507
International politics will disappear once the Empire is established. That day the wind will be heard in the negotiation halls.

~

508
The future is full of wonders. Some of them will be so destructive that they will change the face of this planet.

~

509
There is only one item that humanity cannot live without: water.

~

510
Falling asleep is the best activity of the day.
It feels like a flight towards freedom.

511
We are being served by both angels and devils.
That is why it feels like the ball is always in our court.

~

512
Old thinks it is better than Young.
But Young will make fewer mistakes than Old.

~

513
Wisdom does not come with old age. Rather old age understands it cannot ignore wisdom anymore like the young age.

~

514
Young is an improved version of Old.
However, something is always lost in the process.

~

515
Getting old can be fun.
You just need to not take yourself too seriously.

516
There is nothing more exciting than having a family. This is truly "leaving on the edge". The adrenaline flows like a river.

~

517
Couples should prepare for family life by doing the worst to each other before the kids come.

~

518
When children are born you feel like the luckiest prisoner in the courtyard.

~

519
If you don't want to take care of children do not make them. If you do not make children be prepared to be judged silently by family, society, and later yourself.

~

520
Children are little people that need your resources to survive. And they think you have unlimited resources.

521
The world is a dangerous place when it is not boring.

~

525
Preparing for the future is mostly a futile act since we don't know how it is going to turn out.

~

526
Learning cannot ever be accumulated in high enough quantity.

~

524
Educating oneself is not enough to help the world.
A giving heart is also required.

~

525
This world needs good people to step up.
Bad people are not shy.

526
The sign that our leaders do not care about human life is that there is still wide spread famine in this world.

~

527
If we want our children to be happy we should teach them the value of giving.

~

528
Competition is good only if it is done with a noble goal in sight.

~

529
Remorse is proof that God still thinks we have a chance to change.

~

530
Change for better, even when it is too late, it is still welcomed.

531
Before children want to change the world they already see that there is a problem with it. This should not be so.

~

535
No matter how many questions we answer our children, they will always be curious to see how much we still know.

~

536
If we remove the Caiman Islands and Switzerland from the banking system theoretically that should not lead to World War III.

~

534
In modern times wealth is not measured in how much taxes you pay but in how much you manage to move to offshore accounts.

~

535
If only one of the trillions of dollars hidden from visible economy was to be transformed into food, then world hunger would be solved. If even that is not enough, what does it tell us on the urgency of this matter?

536
Classical music has energies that are unique and hidden. And they will remain hidden until you decide to listen to some of it.

~

537
Slavery, prostitution, exploitation and tyranny are social diseases as old as written history. At some point you start to ask yourself if these are not in fact the moral precepts that a majority of people want to live by.

~

538
People should not complain about work. It is an activity we do for no more than 50 years.

~

539
Today I saw a hawk. He was flying from one tree to another. I got a good look at him since these two trees were the last ones from his once large habitat.

~

540
Scientists say that the ocean does not have enough area that is under protection from us. Lucky for the ocean there are already plans to expand it on all coastal cities due to the higher global temperature.

541
Ocean floors are hidden to our eyes and we cannot see all the horror we caused down there so that we can pretend at least that we want to put the brakes on ocean pollution. But don't worry.
Nature has a plan for us as well.

~

542
Eating worms and frying lizards will be recalled as luxury by the remains of humanity living in a poisoned world.

~

543
This planet is the only thing we can call home for many years to come. And don't dream of any illusion about living on other planets in the next 1000 years or more… or never.

~

544
The most visible achievement of our civilization will be a toxic planet. So much scientific discovery used so wrongly.

~

545
The planet can regenerate but it will need a miracle. From the beginning the game was rigged anyway.

546
Recipe for disaster: Make a planet.
Insert some intelligent beings there.
Watch them overpopulate.

~

547
Miracles happen only when you lose all hope.
If they don't happen even then, than what's the point of their existence?

~

548
The internet is not just a modern tool. It is a true mirror of our soul. And any mirror is a good tool no matter how dirty the images reflected in it.

~

549
Before the Internet, lying was the rule of life for all politicians. After the Internet they do it at their own risk.

~

550
Privacy is as endangered by the Internet as elephants and whales by habitat loss and hunting. All of them will probably not survive this generation.

551
For thousands of years people knew how to live and behave towards one another.
Then the Internet appeared.

~

552
Our children will not know what we mean when we will speak from our experiences.

~

553
Our grandchildren will not know what our children mean when they will speak from experience.

~

554
In three generations from its creation the Internet will disappear. It will be replaced by the Collective Mind, a terrifying creature that cannot be anything but tyrannical.

~

555
If you want to escape civilization you will need to start over in caves. Or else the drones will see you every second.

556
The future is so insecure that you better start to love the present.

~

557
Once you know the future you begin to appreciate History.

~

558
There are too many people on this planet to live in a civilized manner and too few to change this planet for the better.

~

559
What we need is not dreamers but doers that were once dreamers.

~

560
If you love your children teach them how to read books. This is the only skill necessary to rebuild civilization as it was once.

561
You can be a pessimist or an optimist.
Either way, it will not matter when SHTF.
Only pure knowledge will.

~

562
If you need hope look beyond this Universe.

~

563
If you don't need hope, be constructive and give
some to others.

~

564
School will teach you as much as you want to learn
but the great students will always learn after
finishing school.

~

565
If you want to change this world you should first find
into what, with details.

566
If you want to change the world first read history to see if what you propose was not done already.

~

567
Concentrate your positive energy, don't let it spread or it will be ineffective.

~

568
There is a time for despair and a time for hope. Personally I see no negative effect in just skipping the time for despair.

~

569
Once you go fishing for the first time you understand what real freedom means when it's time to go back home.

~

570
Happiness cannot be measured in logical statements because it is coming only from God and He is above logic.

571
Ultimate freedom is when you don't have anything and you do not need anything. Unfortunately, on Earth our stomach makes this state impossible.

~

572
The pursuit of happiness is the only reason we allow ourselves to live.

~

573
Discrimination is a two way road.
However, not all people travel on it.

~

574
The term racism does not show where the problem begins. That is why the term "racism" should be changed to "personal culture clash".

~

575
The cure for racism or social phobias is "live and let live". This is going to work only if all sides have access to unrestrained freedom of speech.

576
It is hate speech only if it's a lie or a half-lie.

~

577
Don't trouble yourself with learning how to drive. Soon all cars will be abandoned either for utopian reasons or for catastrophic reasons.
Try the bicycle.

~

578
Learn how to cook and be open minded about ingredients. The future might teach you something about scarcity.

~

579
If you want to rest eat less or else your body will have to work even when you relax.

~

580
Eating the same food every day is either addiction or poverty.

581
Reading a good book can improve your health even if it is not related to this subject.

~

582
You are as good as your mind. Take care of it and do not subject it to harmful chemicals.

~

583
The body is less important than the mind.
The mind is less important the soul. The soul is less important than being on the right side of history.

~

584
There are multiple points of perspective towards the Truth. But there is only one Truth.

~

585
For an unorganized mind this is an unorganized Universe.

586
You can judge if you're well-dressed based on social factors or weather factors. Choose weather first.

~

587
If you live a promiscuous life then don't worry about the future. You don't have one.

~

588
In times of war we pay attention to many details. In time of peace we should do the same.

~

589
Fitness is the new religion of the body.
And every religion has fanatics.

~

590
Running is not the same as walking and walking is not the same as staying still. Each level counts.

591
All chairs are death traps.
Spend as little time as possible on them.

~

592
The pathway through thoughts often leads to surprising conclusions.

~

593
There are people that see the world differently and there are people that see the world the same. Unless they discuss their views the world will not improve.

~

594
The views that are offensive test the conviction of the views that are not.

~

595
Sleep, eat, think, sleep.
Sleep, eat, think, meditate, sleep.
Sleep, think, eat, meditate, act, sleep.
Sleep, meditate, eat, act, sleep.
Sleep.

596
Meditation is nothing but a word without a clear subject to meditate upon.

~

597
If you meditate do not do it for the benefit of your body. It smells of fake meditation.

~

598
Meditation is a profound way of thinking about existential questions. On any other subject it should be called just "thinking".

~

599
Listening to music or working with your hands is possible while in deep meditation. Sometimes these actions can be the actual trigger of the meditative state.

~

600
The scheming man cannot reach a meditative state. He will always think in the present.

601
Transforming your meditation into an action of some kind is a fortunate conclusion to it.

~

602
Meditation does not bring happiness but it helps in finding it.

~

603
It is said that crazy people don't have enough mind. Actually their mind is chronically overcrowded.

~

604
Disruptive technologies are only disruptive to the biggest exploiters of this world. That is until they can get control of the said technologies.

~

605
Art always helps Economy. However, when it gets the chance Economy does not help Art.

606
Without Art we will live like the dead, blinded to beauty.

~

607
Most artists need to wait a few lives before they can get fully appreciated.
Not so with fake artists.

~

608
Astrology and Alchemy still employ many people, centuries after they were debunked.

~

609
Astrology and Alchemy both tried to make gold out of nothing. Astrology succeeded from the first try and still does it every time today.

~

610
Horror movies differ from historical movies on the fact that they are fake.

611
Comedy movies are not the opposite of horror movies but of drama movies. The opposite of horror movies are religious movies.

~

612
Beautiful movies make you smile while you get sad.

~

613
The journey of life is not about getting wiser.
What we want is to reach the end destination safely.

~

614
If you move against the current you will go forward far less than if you move with it.

~

615
In the end we are all free to do whatever we want.

616
Some of us are in it for the money, some of us are in it for the competition and some are just watching the show meditating on what it all means.

~

617
Philosophers are helpless against the mystery of life. They have something to say only on what to do with it. That is why they are all wrong about it.

~

618
When you make a second step after the first step, it is called progress. With thoughts you need to analyze the third thought before you can say that the second thought constitutes progress from the first thought.

~

619
The inefficiency of philosophers does not come from the systems they are proposing, but from the fact that these systems always change. Some think this is actually their strength. Not me.

~

620
You cannot be all that you can be in one short life. That is why you have to reserve Eternity for this project.

621
If you bet against me that I cannot do it all, I'll match your bet and I'll raise you enough time from Eternity to do it thoroughly.

~

622
There are two ways: you can concentrate on many simple goals at the same time, or you can concentrate on one single complex goal until the end. But if you concentrate on anything you will miss out on what is around you.

~

623
Once you are on top do not forget that everybody sees you now. The least you can do is to give the crowd a show.

~

624
Boring is as boring does.
And chocolate has nothing to do with it.

~

625
If you want to immerse yourself in philanthropy get into cold fusion energy. Even if it fails... what a show! But what if it doesn't fail?

626
Money can clear your reputation pretty fast. It will be temporary though. Better stick with being good.

~

627
Some geniuses are recognized for what they are in their life time. But the majority of geniuses are smart enough to not let the public do that while they live.

~

628
Fear is natural. Trust is also natural.
Make sure stupidity does not switch them at times.

~

629
The Universe is as large as our space phobia.

~

630
Some fear small places, some fear large places.
The Universe is both at the same time.

631
Matter is dancing throughout the Universe in a repetitive melody that receives less and less applause.

~

632
If "God is dead" then why we are still afraid of him? Maybe because we suspect that He is only pretending to be dead.

~

633
Money doesn't exist. It is part of a play game, only on this planet.

~

634
Time travel will be possible only when time will cease to exist.

~

635
You cannot stop Time locally while the Universe goes forward.

636
If we stop Time the Universe ceases to exist, since it is based on continuous movement.

~

637
To stop Time you need as much energy as the entire Universe to counter the forward movement. To reverse Time you will need more energy than that.

~

638
We are time traveling every day.
They are called memories.

~

639
If time travelling will be allowed then we will never have to face consequences for our mistakes.

~

640
Even God never time travelled, although He could. He respects "free will" too much to do it even when He is often annoyed with us.

641
Gravity, Proportions, Time and various Physic Laws are all a construct of One's mind.
What if He changes his mind?

~

642
Being watched it is not the same as being controlled. It gives some stress though.

~

643
There will be one day when outsourcing jobs will stop. You cannot outsource jobs from robots or software.

~

644
The only efficient way forward is a world where there are no more jobs for human beings. However, they will still need to be paid in full.

~

645
If anyone fools himself into believing that poor people will suffer patiently forever, they should read history. That is why I recommend society to get payless before going jobless.

646
Asia, Europe, Africa, both Americas are not continents for the rich. They are districts, so they might as well use numbers for them.

~

647
Running from one continent to another is slowly becoming the only world sport.

~

648
The only thing that is not in short supply on this planet are dreams and hopes.

~

649
In some countries being at the wrong place and at the wrong time is becoming a way of life.

~

650
In the Free World, free speech is getting you punished.

651
The truth might be interpretable but the reality is not.

~

652

Real issues cannot be hidden under the carpet for long. Soon the rug itself will be one giant issue.

~

653
The last future World War "casus belli" will be unavoidable: food & water.

~

654
If all people become vegetarian that will still not stop the disappearance of all animals. It just postpones it until most of the plants are finished off.

~

655

Soon even insects will be endangered due to our daily stomach requirements.

656
Go in the forest, look at a deer. This should be enough to make you an activist for the forests or your grandchild will not have the unique feeling you had in that forest.

~

657
Envision our planet is nothing but one large city. That is the most depressing vision of all and we should fight against it.

~

658
We should speed up and greatly increase the number of our ballistic missiles. Then when all is ready we should send all nuclear weapons towards a safe route outside the solar system.

~

659
No professional army can stand against a "grand army". A "grand army" can be raised only if you credibly propose a better world.

~

660
If we want to have any chance of living in space, we have to establish large moon cities before we deplete most of our planetary resources.

661
We are in a race against time on all personal or general issues. Imagine a world where there is no upper time limit. That's why it is called Heaven.

~

662
Heaven is the hardest religious concept to renounce.

~

663
If you want to forget about God forget first about death. If you want to forget about death forget first about old age. If you want to forget about old age, die young.

~

664
I cannot imagine what Adam's impression was about old age, but something tells me that this is where the first swear words come from. Lots of them.

~

665
Stand-up comedy is still the cheapest form of humor.

666
A comedian should know that in this field of work although everything is permitted not everything is accepted.

~

667
Not only do we have a short life but on top of that it is cut in half by sleep.

~

668
All you need to triple your personal free time is for somebody to invent a machine that let us work in our sleep.

~

669
What we need in our life is purpose to aspire to. Fortunately we can find purpose the moment we lose our selfishness.

~

670
Selfishness is the expression of a chronic lack of empathy. That is what monsters are made of.

671
Charity and volunteering are one and the same virtue. The difference is that one is active and the other is passive.

~

672
Beside the job, food and sleep are the other two barriers against a productive life.

~

673
Even one hour of your life spent on a job cannot be repaid with all the money in the world.
So, one should really value his private time.

~

674
Self-employed sometimes means self-slave.

~

675
Freedom is the most precious gift that God gave to men. And then He took it from us and threw us out of Eden.

676
The angels are the only beings that are free and happy. That is why we picture them as clean, young and flying wherever they want.

~

677
Every internal organ in our body is designed to inflict excruciating and prolonged pain. This cannot be by chance or evolution.

~

678
The proof that we are not on the highest evolution ladder is the lizard. It does not feel enough pain to stop running when it leaves her tail behind. Later it grows back, again with no pain.

~

679
Pain teaches many things. But even with these valuable lessons learned we still feel that the less pain we feel in this life, the better.

~

680
Diseases are not punishments because that will make God too cruel. Think of them instead as disincentives against liking this life too much.

681
Although many melodies will like to be called music, very few are.

~

682
Classical music is the only place where even noise is musical.

~

683
Classical music instruments differ from the modern instruments in that they can sing in tune with each other even when used in great numbers.

~

684
The beauty and mystery of classical music is that it uses the material world to create pure spiritual world.

~

685
Every person that wants to listen to classic music should start listening to pieces close to their heart and grow from there.

686
After many years of listening to both classic music and modern music I can clearly say that if I will be given a second chance I will not lose my time with modern music. At all!

~

687
If I will be given the choice to learn life either through books or through music I will chose music. That will guarantee having a happier soul.

~

688
There is no concept of a lie in music.

~

689
Mental prison is the only prison.

~

690
What happens in prison is a raw version of what happens outside prison.

691
Prison mentality is what our leaders want us to acquire, since our freedom is their only enemy.

~

692
Every institution, every collective is a prison of some kind. You ignore the rules at your peril.

~

693
This planet is rapidly becoming a large prison yard. It didn't start that way.

~

694
The only free person is the one that does not care about this world.

~

695
The moment you get attached by any part of this material world, you will have the same fate of a fly caught in a carnivorous follower.

696
When in prison, use the time in your favour.
Do not let the time use you.

~

697
There is no prison. It is just you, alive and kicking in a smaller world.

~

698
Memories are laced with melancholy.

~

699
Living in the past is the past time of a quitter.

~

700
Melancholy can be equally destructive or useful when used for future decisions.

701
Our memories give value to our life.
Create as many good ones as possible.

~

702
Creating memories is like manufacturing any other product. It takes energy, time and investment.

~

703
You can either invest your energy in your life or in other people's life. Either way it is a shame to just store this energy.

~

704
Holidays are a time of rejoicing. If you need me to tell you that then you have deep problems that you should address immediately.

~

705
There is absolutely nothing special about a holiday unless you make it so.

706
There are many holidays in a year.
Chose at least three and make them extra special.

~

707
Combining stinginess with celebration is like
combining water with fire.

~

708
Holidays are magic days for children.
Treat them like that as well when you are an adult.

~

709
Get with the program and smile.
It will not hurt you. Same with kindness.

~

710
Holidays are the worst time to introduce the concept
of money to young children.

711
There is no special Holiday.
There is no ordinary day either.

~

712
Any day is special.
You just didn't get the memo yet.

~

713
Cold or warm, happy or unhappy, poor or rich are
just relative personal conclusions.

~

714
The reason you cannot find love in this world is
because you did not recognize it so many times.

~

715
Go and spread love and kindness.
Somebody will take notice and change as well.

716
Goodness is the only sign you are not selfish.

~

717
Rather than give money, give yourself.
It is more pleasant for the receivers.

~

718
Business decisions are like war decisions.
They feel justified until you see the results.

~

719
The only permanent good business decisions are the ones that ultimately benefit the whole world.

~

720
Doing business is as general concept as breathing.
Both can be used for good or evil.

721
Charity is good business practice.
If you do not know that, than your "business" is just another predatory activity.

~

722
Some business men cut Charity work from their companies thinking that this "goodwill" virtue somehow is part of the diminishable workforce. That is the *apple* of discord between them and the world.

~

723
Taking pleasure in giving is reserved only for the happiest people on Earth.

~

724
Holiness is where sky and earth meet without fighting each other.

~

725
Few people think holiness is achievable in life.
That is exactly who has a chance to achieve it.

726

In old religions or even in the new ones like atheism, there is a spirit of giving. Some give more importance to it than others.

~

727

Agnosticism is short way of saying that you might believe in something if you will want to.

~

728

The difference between an atheist and an agnostic is that one is a believer while the other doesn't want to be bothered with religious questions.

~

729

The only difference between an atheist and a religious person is in what God they believe in.

~

730

The most focused on the material world between an atheist and an agnostic is the latter, since he is the only one that is not concerned at all with religion.

731
Beyond death there is something, or else nothing before death will really matter.

~

732
Without life after death there is no concept of freedom. Our own personal prison, *the body* is enough proof of this.

~

733
If you want to focus on this world I suggest you do it in the next 70-90 years of your life. If you want to focus on the next world you have an infinite time at your disposal.

~

734
Religious ideas are always sharp. That is because they need to cut to the heart of the problem.

~

735
If you ask a politician if God exists wait until he is firmly in power so that he can answer you:
Now he does exist.

736
There are dangerous ideas and less dangerous ideas. There is no such thing as a harmless idea.

~

737
Danger can be defined in relation with the object you want the most to protect: body or soul.

~

738
You cannot protect your body indefinitely. Ultimately, it dies.

~

739
There are people that know they will die and other people that believe they will never die. Who do you want to be?

~

740
There are people that believe they will die and other people that know they will never die. Who do you want to be?

741
The ones that are staying in a "No Man's Land" are in more danger than the ones that chose a side, since their numbers are few.

~

742
If you chose yourself over another better be sure that you did it for something good or you just condemned yourself.

~

743
3000 years ago an Egyptian aristocrat painted an account of his massive fortune on a wall. That is the only thing that remained from it.

~

744
If you build an empire don't forget to name it or later nobody will ever remember that it even existed.

~

745
Very few emperors are remembered with admiration. Very few artists are remembered with disdain.

746
Emperors are remembered well only because of artists and writers.

~

747
True artists are all equal.
They all shared their gifts with the world.

~

748
Science and Art are the same thing. One searches for beauty, the other for usefulness. When they work together the product is whole.

~

749
There is much creativity involved in science. Technology is our way of organizing and using the energy of the Universe.

~

750
An inventor is somebody that for the most part does not believe the schoolbooks.

751
All science schoolbooks contain lies. How many lies and which ones, only the future will determine.

~

752
Sometimes lazy people's wishes improve our world more than active people's wishes.

~

753
Solving problems requires creativity. Creativity requires free thoughts. Thinking requires spending less time working. Sometimes better productivity is not what a company needs.

~

754
A company that has a better idea for channeling a pathway from its employees to managements will always think fresh.

~

755
Productivity is sometimes managed by the most unproductive members of society.

756
From all artists one in particular is the least loved by both rulers and people: the Comic. However his creation is highly appreciated.

~

757
A good photographic image can give us the same feeling as a painting, but not the same value.

~

758
Photography is the art with the cheapest investment in time versus great results.

~

759
Showing the beauty of this world was never easier than today, with the advent of digital photography.

~

760
People need solitude more than noise. The mind wants to be able to hear itself so it can see further.

761
At any point in your life you can consider yourself a failure as well as a success. Choosing between these two extreme conclusions boils down to mood.

~

762
If you find yourself with nothing in this world but a cheerful attitude, then consider your life a success.

~

763
Success is paid in multiple failures.

~

764
There are seven letters in both of these words: success, failure. If it is all equal to you, then go with success.

~

765
Ice is water with air bubbles in it. Such is your life, full of random meaningless decisions. Some ice cubes look clearer than others.

766
If you want to love, you can do it immediately.
If you want to be loved prepare to wait.

~

767
In an evil world being good is harder than being bad.
In a good world, it is the same.

~

768
The birds sing for free. If they eat your food it does not mean they accepted a payment since they believe food is free also.

~

769
Children and animals don't know of money.
That is why they keep asking for the desired object and do not understand why our heart does not feel the same as theirs.

~

770
Ducks, gooses and swans do not know which one of them is more beautiful. We think we do.
They are right and we are wrong.

771
All creatures respect each other. We are the only ones that do not respect the others or even us.

~

772
Our brain interprets tastes for what they are not: punishments and rewards.

~

773
Sleep is just another fake obstacle that was inserted into our life in order to show us "how human" we are.

~

774
Our body is an ally of a shadow warrior.
If we want to defeat that warrior we must become almost as thin as a shadow.

~

775
Rest does not come from sleep.
But sleep helps facilitate it from time to time.

776
There is no real rest for the living.

~

777
Some rest can be achieved with great costs or just by waiting long enough.

~

778
Global warming is a hot topic these days.

~

779
At one point in the future the majority of people will renounce meat, not long after they have renounced vegetables.

~

780
We should think proactively and start building sooner than later those flood-earthquake-tornado proof houses.

781
The only global action happening now is theft.

~

782
Soon global warming will be literally our last concern.

~

783
The optimists will always take all that is good from life leaving all that is bad for the pessimists.

~

784
If you want to become an optimist, you are already one.

~

785
All planets have planetary problems.
Only for Pluto the problems are dwarfed.

786
Destruction is mesmerizing.
That is why we love to see comets.

~

787
There is destruction hidden in wealth.
But it can be creatively managed.

~

788
Rich people often have poor children.

~

789
The cure for rich disease is temporary poverty plus some culture.

~

790
If you are rich and can't be a Michelangelo, at least be a Maecenas. If you don't know who Maecenas is, please learn so you can be helpful.

791
Rich kids are often more destructive than their rich parents.

~

792
Wealth comes and goes like the sea. Charity is like an anchor protecting you from getting swept away.

~

793
Wealth is for the wise what clay is for a sculptor.

~

794
A sculptor, a painter and a musician look at a saint and get inspired.

~

795
Heroes are born by looking at martyrs.

796
Leaders are constructed by people's grievous needs.

~

797
Tyrants are made by themselves.

~

798
Slaves are made by their initial inability to quickly become killers.

~

799
Normal people are made by normal circumstances. Extraordinary circumstances will show that some of those people are extraordinary.

~

800
Remove normality from people's lives and they will show who they really are.

801
Geniuses are put in this world to show the others that they are losing their time pursuing artistic or scientific perfection.

~

802
If you want to know what man can do, look towards geniuses. For what we are actually doing look at the history books.

~

803
Both the genius and the good hearted village idiot impress people with their raw humanity.

~

804
Occasionally the good-hearted village idiot happens to also be a genius. That's when people can't stand to be near him anymore.

~

805
The genius never looks down on the village idiot because he notices the identical stare they both receive from people.

806
Normality is what others want from you.
The best you can do in this life is to surprise them.

~

807
If you want to go beyond your limits do not set up
any or you might "chicken out".

~

808
Limits are a safety net. You can sleep on a safety net
or use it to jump as high as you can.

~

809
If you follow your dream, one day you might have a
rude awakening. Still, that is better than to wake up
before dreaming.

~

810
When it is about your dream, allow yourself to make
mistakes without despairing.

811
Do not choose between dreams.
Try them all at least once.

~

812
We can see proofs of heaven and hell throughout our entire lives.

~

813
The difference between love and passion is that there is respect to be found in love, among many other amazing treats.

~

814
Love encompasses passion, but passion does not encompass love.

~

815
The reason a lover sees his loved one differently than others is because the others are blind to reality.

816
A man can love any woman and a woman can love any man. Only marriage can stop this madness successfully.

~

817
Passion can hurt you more than war. And there is no protection against it besides religious values.

~

818
Intimacy is required by passion and not by love.

~

819
The reason God asked for more love than one has for their family is because He knows just how much family abuse there is in this world.

~

820
Most of the time your wife's or husband behaviour is nothing more than a mirror of your own actions. And like any mirror it can be used to correct yourself, or not.

821
If you want to emerge victorious in a fight with your wife or husband, look beyond the winning argument.

~

822
The harmony of a couple is protected by the spontaneity of the relationship.

~

823
Boredom is as unpleasant in two as it is in one.

~

824
It is said that the opposites attract. This is true only if they meet in the middle from time to time.

~

825
Being in love is like the Sky and the Ocean. You don't know where one ends or where the other starts.

826
If you are extreme in your love, the other might mistake this for a condition you might have.

~

827
There is no possession in love.
However that might not be its strength.

~

828
Marriage with love is the closest thing to a perfect relationship.

~

829
The only reason why Adam was not visibly and ceremoniously married with Eve, is because they were the only human beings around. So no protection was required yet.

~

830
Marriage is actually a contract between the couple and all others.

831
Your marriage is not a car. So if you want to fix it do not kick it, contrary to your first impulse.

~

832
There is nothing more misleading than a man fighting with his wife. You might think erroneously that they do not love each other.

~

833
Love is the simplest thing in the world.
It becomes complex only because of the world.

~

834
Love is about spending all of your time acknowledging each other.

~

835
Love does not have an opposite because nothing can equal love.

836
True love can exist only between you and the entire humanity. The rest of the feelings are just poor copies that can mimic love for one person or another.

~

837
"Love your enemy" is linked directly to the acknowledgement that the whole humanity is our sibling.

~

838
"Normality" is the only word in our vocabulary that we are not sure what it stands for.

~

839
Charity to the undeserving is a gate to their heart.

~

840
Government cuts from the vulnerable to protect the powerful. It sounds crazy until you learn who government is really working for.

841
The treatment of the poor, artists, the physically or mentally impaired, the addicted and diseased is the true measure of Nations or entire Civilizations.

~

842
Since the Dawn of Man people lived in a constant Oligarchy sprinkled from time to time with Tyranny.

~

843
What was once the floor of the sea it is now the desert of the Sahara. Time is sculpting every day and we don't even notice.

~

844
Time will never stop.
The Universe will end.
We will not.

~

845
Time was invented so that we can be taught humility, not destruction.

846
We can think that we were made for the Universe or that the Universe was made for us. Only one side can be right about this.

~

847
Science magnified our view of the changes in this Universe, answering many "How's". But to find the answer to "Why's", you need to die first.

~

848
People concentrate on "Now" moments more than they should. Let's not forget that "Now" just passed and "Forever" is still in front of us.

~

849
If you don't believe in "Forever", then you should never use the word. However, the word exists for a reason.

~

850
"Forever" scares people out of their wits.
That is because they don't like themselves much.

851
If there is not a "Beyond" life, then we do not need to worry about the present life either, since the consequences will not last much.

~

852
Hope is a word linked to "Beyond" and "Forever". It cannot exist in a time limited world.

~

853
Justice is an atemporal concept like Happiness or Truth.

~

854
How can you be truly happy knowing this happiness will eventually end? True Happiness needs "Forever" in order to exist.

~

855
Pleasurable can be mistaken with happiness by people that don't believe in "Beyond" and "Forever".

856
Time's lessons take too much time to be useful in a time limited life. Maybe the conclusions are for later.

~

857
If you concentrate on this life you might lose the next one.

~

858
"Next Life" is a subject of great interest for everybody that wants to live.

~

859
Clinging to this life is for the weak. We are all weak, but occasionally some of us get stronger.

~

860
We can survive only for a while, or we can start living "Forever" now.

861
Correctness, mercy, goodness, respectfulness, integrity and other virtues are a hindrance in a time-limited and unjust world. Still, they must be valued by us for a different reason.

~

862
Virtues are useful only in a timeless life.

~

863
The Universe is too large to be managed only by laws. It needs an Enforcer as well.

~

864
The laws of the Universe are flexible in certain conditions. The more we know about them the more flexible they get.

~

865
If it looks like Magic it probably is, even if it is explained by Science.

866
Magic and Science both talk of laws.

~

867
Science is not omnipotent.
And we really like the concept of Omnipotence.
It gives us peace of mind.

~

868
Great Minds have better chances to become Great Souls. But they often don't use these chances.

~

869
Heroes fight when there is a chance to win. Great Heroes fight even when there is no chance to win and they often become Martyrs.

~

870
Going all in is the most exhilarating experience when it is for a just cause.

871
What is unjust cannot be just no matter how many people are doing it.

~

872
Killing and maiming are virtues only for the cruel. Empathy shames them.

~

873
You do not need to kill to achieve immortality. No matter what you do, Immortality is waiting to snatch you the moment you die.

~

874
Justice is not forever postponed. It just gives you enough time to prosecute you forever.

~

875
Nobody can fool anybody for long.
After a while they all pretend and wait patiently for the end of the lie.

876

You cannot have true justice in this world.
That will require prosecuting everybody.

~

877

Ozymandias is known not for his works but for his foolishness.

~

878

The Fool, the Smart, the Wiseman and the Inspired gathered to share experiences.
The Fool did not listen to anybody.
The Smart thought he was right.
The Wise knew he did not know anything.
The Inspired did most of the talking.

~

879

The boats were moored on the lake for many years.
One was sunken in the lake.
One was half sunken and was green with moss.
One was afloat, still chained to the pole.
One was in the middle of the lake enjoying its long fight with the winds and the waves.

~

880

The birds went to sing in the middle of the forest.
Animals were listening.
Hawks were looking.
Worms were resting.

881
Protect your energy for the battles ahead.
Do not forget to use it though.

~

882
Popsicles, wealth and power melt away. Fighting for them seems such a loss of good energy. Still, almost everybody does it for some misunderstood reasons.

~

883
For each billionaire there are one million people starving, usually because of them.

~

884
Making wealth is not a crime. Ditching taxes and moving wealth in off-shore accounts is. Based on this equation, how many of the rich are not criminals? Depends on what laws they made for themselves.

~

885
Sooner than later all the rich will need more than private airplanes to move around.
Private armies will be required.

886
The most spiritual thought a billionaire is capable of seeing is himself paying all his taxes.

~

887
Before becoming very rich the businessman requires one special surgery: cutting his umbilical cord with humanity.

~

888
Tyrants are rich people that are visible to the world. However, there are many rich people whom the world does not see yet.

~

889
The rich take great care of their public face since it's their only human aspect.

~

890
There is no shortage of food.
Only a chronic shortage of good will.

891
All movie superheroes do is beat the small time thugs and fall in love. In real life they will go straight for the top thugs and not stop until they clean this planet entirely.

~

892
After so many movies with Superman we can conclude that he is either lazy or evil. How else can we explain at the end of it all that the planet has the same poverty and injustice issues as in his first movie?

~

893
We are living on a planet full of villains and super-villains, where the only superhero we know is gone for an indefinite time. Some lost hope he will return, some are still hoping.

~

894
The night is dark and we are darker.
But the light is just an eyelid away.
Sometimes we can even see it through our eyelids.

~

895
The storm passes with no regard to the damages it causes. First you rebuild in your head, then you rebuild outside.

896
Change is expected by some, desired by many, and reviled by few here.

~

897
The tree loses its leaves one by one during the many days of Fall. But when the big storm comes all the leaves fall in a matter of minutes.

~

898
All the leaves, no matter how much they fly, will end up eventually on the ground.

~

899
You will miss Nature.
Nature will not miss you.

~

900
What you have in common with Nature is that both of you don't like Time.

901
Time is the only component that is truly invisible in this Universe.

~

902
Because we assume Time exists we invented laws for it.

~

903
Time is as ephemeral as Nature. Only somebody that is not ephemeral can observe this.

~

904
The difference between ephemeral and eternal is not shown by Time but by what is real.

~

905
Reality cannot be changed by appearances no matter how visible they are.

906
We can identify as appearances the objects or situations that do not endure eternally.

~

907
Time and time again we are attracted by Reality no matter how incredible it is.

~

908
Appearances fight us on the way to Reality.

~

909
Who doesn't know already what Reality is lives in a painful state of questions with no satisfying answers.

~

910
The pink slip is the corporation's way of softening the blow. This policy is insensitive to color blind employees.

911
The crocodile, the iguana and the Komodo dragon think they are part of the survivors club. But the small lizard knows that Nature is always on the look out to downsize.

~

915
The fly on the wall is rewarded with honey in governments and corporations, instead of being swatted back to toilet.

~

913
The lioness does all the work while the lion doesn't move a claw. However he is not lazy, always fighting other lions for the top position.

~

914
"Live and let live" is somewhat changed in the corporate culture with "live and you are let go".

~

915
What is the fighting about in Star Wars movies other than a theological struggle? The West renamed its old faith and business bloomed.

916
The Jedi looks, feels and talks like Franciscan monks. This is because the West never ever lost its faith. And with Disney's blessing, it never will.

~

917
Planet X will be the 9th planet to be discovered. For Pluto "lost in translation" is an understatement.

~

918
Planet Three is our home.
Planet Four is our job.
Planet X is our curiosity.
But the Universe is so large that by the time we finish to explore it, all these Planets will be long lost memories.

~

919
Each human being is one Universe.
Each Universe is as valuable as the next one.
All Universes must be experienced, but you need an Eternity to do it. We are in luck.

~

920
A baby becomes a child that becomes an adult which in time becomes an Angel and further on becomes an Archangel.

921
A baby becomes a child that becomes an adult which in time becomes old and soon becomes nothing.

~

922
No matter what physical activities you are engaged in, they will all amount to a pile of dust on a dune in some desert, just before becoming glass due to the heat coming from the explosion of the Sun.

~

923
All atoms in this Universe are to be disassembled. What is our plan beyond that?

~

924
The world's color issues will not change significantly until either we are all of mixed races or only of one race.

~

925
19th century was Darwinian.
20th century was Kafkian.
21st century will be Babylonian.
22nd century will be Survivalist.

~

926
In an unthinkable world the machines will do all the thinking.

~

927
Between a machine and a human being the only one that is actually thinking is the human being.
The machine only reacts according to program.

~

928
In the 19th and 20th century humanity was afraid of an alien invasion. In 21st century humanity is ambivalent to such an invasion. By 22nd century we will all be looking forward to it as our last hope to survive.

~

929
The reason we were not contacted by any aliens yet is because there is a space sign above Earth saying: Buyer Beware. Human infested area!

~

930
A reputed scientist said that if we are the only living creatures, then the Universe is an "awful waste of space". Thousands of barren planets found around us seem to enforce the idea that an "awful waste of space" is not such an oddity in the Universe.

931
Looking at how we treat the diversity of species on our native planet, someone might question what is the real reason behind looking for life on other planets? Certainly, not to preserve it...

~

935
Between a forever icy winter and a never ending scorching summer there were two other seasons but I forgot their names.

~

933
The Internet of Things will make detective work almost impossible since there will be too many variables to take into account when investigating clues through regular object usage.

~

934
As our lives become more digital, our defining thoughts will get buried behind mountains of useless information.

~

935
New technologies are the heralds of a new crisis.

~

936
Sooner than later all of us will be clueless when talking about modern technologies.

~

937
The defining moments in all recorded history of the last five thousand years will be just blimps compared to what is coming in the next few generations.

~

938
History will repeat itself less and less due to our greater and greater population numbers.

~

939
If hope disappears from our future we should look in our past to find it again.

~

940
All ideologies are flawed.
All minds are corrupted.
All thought is repetitive.
But Grace is still around here to teach us.

941
Some old books will still be useful to warm our hearts. Many new books will be useful to warm our rooms.

~

942
Diversity is great and it is the first lesson of Creation. The second lesson is that it is not irreplaceable.

~

943
The violinist sings.
The artist paints.
Sounds and colors can dance with each other in our soul.

~

944
There are two roles in a movie: the lead role and the good role. One depends on luck, the other on skill.

~

945
Family gives incredible strength to all generations involved in it.

946
Family is defined by love.
Love is defined by duty.

~

947
We are not defined by the sum of all our activities.
We can still change for better or for worse at any
point in time.

~

948
The level of our complexity can be enhanced by our
simplicity.

~

949
A shepherd on the mountain projects a clearer
direction to his scared sheep than a CEO to his
employees. At least the sheep know that the wolf is
on their back and not in front of them pretending to
lead.

~

950
What is expensive in this world is not life but the
luxuries that surround it.

951
Almost all our time is lost by our desire for stability.

~

952
All we need to do to be free is to accept it.

~

953
We call "Life" the time we manage while waiting for real Freedom, which will come only "After".

~

954
Better to not exist than to just stick around in an aimless Universe.

~

955
Even Heaven will be a sad place if there is no upward evolution there.

956
Any human being needs at least two things to be happy: stability and change.

~

957
Stability and change can be opposites or they can work together like a Swiss watch.

~

958
Stability and continuity can be opposites or work together like a Swiss watch.

~

959
Art is about change of perspective points so that you learn more.

~

960
Although most perspective points are changeable, some are not.

961
Aristotle was looking for a stable point to move the world. The most visible stable point around us is Eternity. We should build on that.

~

962
The least visible stable point is God.
That is why faith is the first required step to even consider his existence.

~

963
Faith is like a telescope.
More faith makes God more visible.
Less faith makes you more visible.

~

964
There is no such thing as being absolutely faithless. In any person there are always degrees of faith to work with.

~

965
Faith can fade in almost without awareness, like the clear slow sunrise or it can explode like a supernova in your mind and soul.

966
Faith does not lead automatically to action. It can linger all your life without any meaningful results.

~

967
Positive change is based on active decisions. Those decisions can lead to more decisions of the same sort or higher levels.

~

968
We are never at the same level.
We are either going actively up or down in a struggle between our old and new acquired principles.

~

969
Acquiring new principles is required in order to evolve. Testing the old principles will lead to keeping them or discarding them on the side of the road.

~

970
At any point in your life and depending on your inner laziness level you can:
Lose good principles and acquire bad principles.
Keep or lose bad principles and acquire worse principles.
Keep bad principles and acquire good principles.
Lose bad principles and acquire good principles.
Keep good principles and acquire more good principles.
Lose good principles and acquire better principles.

971
Acquiring new principles is done by acquiring new information in the various forms it is presented to you. However, from the same information you can extract an equally number of opposite bad and good principles.

~

972
Good principles are already instilled in you since they are based on logic and perfection that works every time.
Bad principles are based on exaggeration and losing touch with reality.

~

973
Reality is more complex than what our eyes see at a certain point in time and from our limited point of view.

~

974
Behind every tree there can be danger or opportunity. Or it can be nothing at all.

~

975
Our mind is our friend only if it is friendly to others.

976
You cannot find love in the entire Universe if you are full of hate. First you have to empty your hate.

~

977
Love does not come close to hate.
But it can wait around.

~

978
Hate consumes your opportunity of any satisfaction like fire consumes wood. In the end both fire and wood disappear without a trace.

~

979
All you need is not love. It is to be loved.
So don't go looking for it. Just create it.

~

980
There are two kinds of extreme books:
boring ones and life changing ones.
The boring ones should be burned and everything in between should be left to be read after this life. The life changing ones should be read many times over.

981
There is pleasure in reading. There is more pleasure in dreaming about what you've read. But satisfaction starts only when doing what you are dreaming about.

~

982
Do not be all you can be.
Choose carefully what you will be.

~

983
Protect yourself from yourself. Hire yourself a bodyguard from outside you.

~

984
It is not good to respect all your rules no matter what. Some of them might be wrong. Some of them might be too right.

~

985
Balance is the great harmonizer. It can even bring good and evil together for the benefit of both.

986
The benefit of evil is less evil, not more.

~

987
The relationship between Good and Evil is not the same as between Good and Bad. Bad can sometimes plead ignorance.

~

988
Good existed since forever.
Some Good turned to Evil by choice.
Evil turned more Good to Bad by lies.
But some Bad will turn back to Good.
Evil and the rest of Bad will disappear.
Good will exist forever.

~

989
Good has good reasons. Bad can sometimes have good reasons too. Evil has no good or bad reasons since it is the absence of reason itself. However, Evil still have the choice to reason.

~

990
Reason is a mind tool so that we can know what is good from what is bad. We can misinterpret it sometimes and it can lead to what is bad. But for us to become evil, we have to purposely lose entirely the ability to reason.

991

If you give yourself enough time to reason, in the end you will find what is good. If you don't give yourself time to reason good or bad will have no real meaning for you anymore.

~

992

When you reach certain important life conclusions you cannot be sure of their validity until you find somebody that convinces you. There is only One that can successfully do that. All others are unsure.

~

993

You can either try to ask God if your conclusions are good or just draw your conclusions based on His already known conclusions.

~

994

Our priorities should be based on practicality with a pinch of eternity.

~

995

If your values contradict other people's values all you need to do is wait long enough to see who is right.

996
This world's worth is meaningless in the next one, since all the rules will change.

~

997
You are always welcome to live for the moment. But it is a short moment indeed.

~

998
Fire and water are made from the exact same energy and matter.
Only creatures see the differences based on the situation of having different bodily sensor reactions to them.

~

999
Our bodily sensors are telling the truth and lying to us at the same time for each experience we have.
This was done to us for the same reason that we have moral dilemmas:
testing, testing and more testing.

~

1000
Our main dilemma is not if we exist or not. Nor is it if we should be good or bad. The problem in front of us is much more important than reaching any of those trivial conclusions.

Conclusion

We are called from Chaos and Nothingness to stand forever in front of ALL THAT IS. This is too much to bear for some of us and we are looking for a way out in a time-limited dream world that does not really exist.

~

Conclusion

What we are experiencing right now is already the past. The future is our forever present. Any decision we make against the future for the sake of the past will already hurt this present.

~

Conclusion

If we stay focused on the Future we will never miss it.

~

Conclusion

The Past, the Present, and the Future form the gate to Forever.

~

Conclusion

Forever is our only Home.

The End

Front Cover Illustration:
"View from Santorini Island"
photo by Catalin Damir

Back Cover Illustration:
"View from Jamaica"
photo by Catalin Damir

**Book Cover Design
by Catalin Damir**

First Edition 2018

ISBN-13: 978-0-9920635-4-2

ISBN-10: 0992063504

www.ingramcontent.com/pod-product-compliance
Lightning Source LLC
Chambersburg PA
CBHW031348040426
42444CB00005B/227